Birds of Prey

Published by Wildlife Education, Ltd.
9820 Willow Creek Road, Suite 300, San Diego, California 92131

ISBN 1-888153-51-2

Birds of Prey

Created and Written by
John Bonnett Wexo

Scientific Consultant

Arthur Crane Risser, Ph.D.
Curator of Birds
San Diego Zoo

Art Credits

Pages Six and Seven: Kenneth and Robert Goldman; **Pages Eight and Nine:** Kenneth Goldman; **Pages Ten and Eleven:** Kenneth Goldman; **Pages Twelve and Thirteen:** Kenneth and Robert Goldman; **Pages Sixteen and Seventeen:** Richard Oden; **Pages Eighteen and Nineteen:** Richard Oden.

Photographic Credits

Front Cover: Leonard Lee Rue III *(Tom Stack & Assoc.);* **Page Ten: Top Left,** David Siddon; **Middle Left,** Tom McHugh *(Photo Researchers);* **Bottom Left,** David Siddon; **Bottom Right,** C.B. Frith *(Bruce Coleman, Inc.);* **Page Eleven: Top Left,** Kenneth Fink *(Photo Researchers);* **Top Right,** David Siddon; **Middle,** Tom Myers *(Photo Researchers);* **Bottom Left,** Zig Leszczynski *(Animals Animals);* **Pages Fourteen and Fifteen:** Wendy Shattil & Robert Rozinski *(Tom Stack & Assoc.);* **Pages Sixteen and Seventeen:** Ron Austing *(Bruce Coleman, Inc.);* **Page Nineteen:** Zig Leszczynski *(Animals Animals);* **Pages Twenty and Twenty-one:** Robert W. Hernandez *(Photo Researchers);* **Pages Twenty-two and Twenty-three:** Hans & Judy Beste *(Animals Animals).*

Our Thanks To: Charles L. Bieler; Richard L. Binford; Ron Garrison; Andrew Grant; Susan Hathaway; Richard Herczog; Marcia Hobbs; Dr. Charles A. McLaughlin; William Noonan; John Ochse; Dr. Amadeo Rea; Barbara Sallar; Dr. Warren Thomas; Carole Towne; and Lynnette M. Wexo.

Special Thanks To: John W. Anderson

Contents

IMPERIAL EAGLE
Aquila heliaca

MARTIAL EAGLE
Polemaetus bellicosus

STELLER'S SEA EAGLE
Haliaetus pelagicus

HARPY EAGLE
Harpia harpyja

BALD EAGLE
Haliaetus leucocephalus

GOLDEN EAGLE
Aquila chrysaetos

BLACK VULTURE
Coragyps atratus

EGYPTIAN VULTURE
Neophron percnopterus

PALM-NUT VULTURE
Gypohierax angolensis

TURKEY VULTURE
Cathartes aura

KING VULTURE
Sarcoramphus papa

HOODED VULTURE
Necrosyrtes monachus

CALIFORNIA CONDOR
Gymnogyps californianus

WHITE-CHINNED OWL
Pulsatrix koeniswaldiana

LONG-EARED OWL
Asio otus

PONDICHERRY VULTURE
Sarcogyps calvus

Birds of Prey come in a very wide range of sizes, shapes, and colors. There are about 420 different kinds of birds included in the group. Most of them are falcons, eagles, hawks, and vultures. But 139 different kinds of owls are also included.

The smallest bird of prey, the Bornean falconet, weighs about one ounce and is less than six inches long. The largest is the Andean condor, which can weigh almost 30 pounds and have a wing span of over ten feet.

Members of the group are found on every continent. They live in dense tropical jungles and high up in the world's tallest mountains. Some of them live to be very old. One Andean condor is known to have lived 72 years.

6

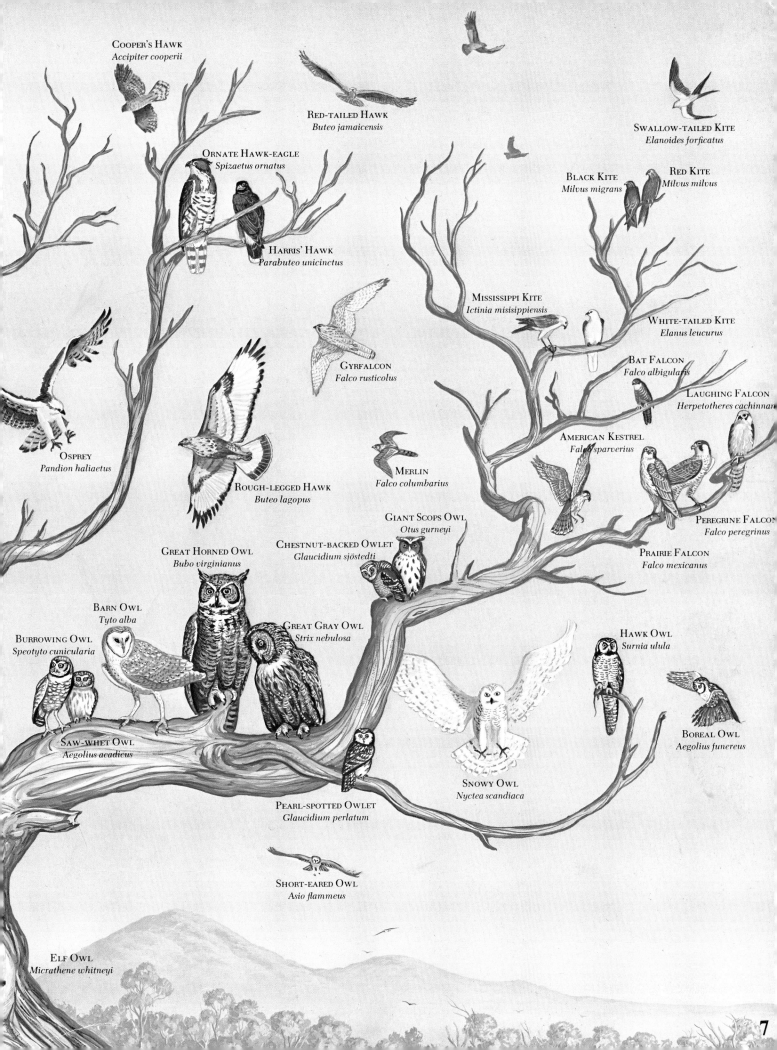

COOPER'S HAWK
Accipiter cooperii

RED-TAILED HAWK
Buteo jamaicensis

SWALLOW-TAILED KITE
Elanoides forficatus

ORNATE HAWK-EAGLE
Spizaetus ornatus

HARRIS' HAWK
Parabuteo unicinctus

BLACK KITE
Milvus migrans

RED KITE
Milvus milvus

MISSISSIPPI KITE
Ictinia misisippiensis

WHITE-TAILED KITE
Elanus leucurus

BAT FALCON
Falco albigularis

GYRFALCON
Falco rusticolus

LAUGHING FALCON
Herpetotheres cachinnan

AMERICAN KESTREL
Falco sparverius

OSPREY
Pandion haliaetus

MERLIN
Falco columbarius

ROUGH-LEGGED HAWK
Buteo lagopus

PEREGRINE FALCON
Falco peregrinus

GIANT SCOPS OWL
Otus gurneyi

CHESTNUT-BACKED OWLET
Glaucidium sjöstedti

PRAIRIE FALCON
Falco mexicanus

GREAT HORNED OWL
Bubo virginianus

BARN OWL
Tyto alba

GREAT GRAY OWL
Strix nebulosa

HAWK OWL
Surnia ulula

BURROWING OWL
Speotyto cunicularia

BOREAL OWL
Aegolius funereus

SAW-WHET OWL
Aegolius acadicus

SNOWY OWL
Nyctea scandiaca

PEARL-SPOTTED OWLET
Glaucidium perlatum

SHORT-EARED OWL
Asio flammeus

ELF OWL
Micrathene whitneyi

The Superb Hunters

The types of birds that are grouped together as Birds of Prey are sometimes very different from each other. Owls, for example, are built differently from hawks and eagles. And they hunt at night, while hawks and eagles are daytime hunters. But the differences seem unimportant compared to the one great skill all birds of prey have in common — their ability to take live prey. Other birds may hunt, but none are nearly as good at it as the birds of prey.

9

PRAIRIE FALCON   *Falco mexicanus*

HARPY EAGLE   *Harpia harpyja*

PYGMY OWL
Glaucidium gnoma

Aristocrats of the Air

Birds of prey are among the most beautiful and impressive creatures on earth. Their piercing eyes, sharp beaks, and strong talons are part of an image of noble power that people have found inspiring throughout history.

MONKEY-EATING EAGLE   *Pithecophaga jefferyi*

BLACK EAGLE   *Aquila verreauxi*

BALD EAGLE
Haliaetus leucocephalus

GOLDEN EAGLE   *Aquila chrysaetos*

LONG-EARED OWL   *Asio otus*

The Anatomy of Flight

The main flight muscles are attached to the big breastbone. These muscles do most of the work when the bird takes off, maneuvers, hovers, or lands.

Birds of prey are often spectacular fliers. Some of them can soar to great heights. And some can plummet through the air at more than 80 miles per hour.

All birds fly in two basic ways—by flapping their wings and by gliding. Birds of prey have very strong flight muscles to help them fly when carrying prey. An eagle can fly with prey that weighs as much as it does.

The big broad wings of eagles, vultures, and buzzards provide maximum lift. This allows the larger birds to fly for long periods without moving their wings.

The short and rather stubby wings of many hawks and some owls provide a lot of lift with some speed. They are good for maneuvering among trees in the forest.

The thin wings of falcons and other small birds of prey are built for speed.

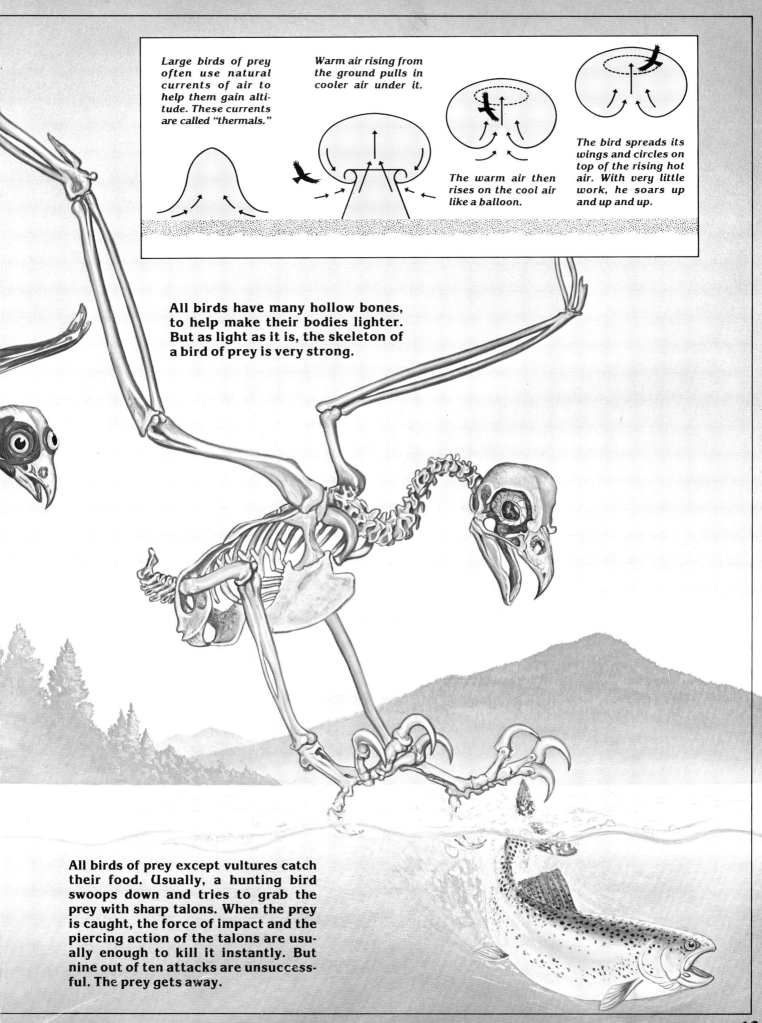

Large birds of prey often use natural currents of air to help them gain altitude. These currents are called "thermals."

Warm air rising from the ground pulls in cooler air under it.

The warm air then rises on the cool air like a balloon.

The bird spreads its wings and circles on top of the rising hot air. With very little work, he soars up and up and up.

All birds have many hollow bones, to help make their bodies lighter. But as light as it is, the skeleton of a bird of prey is very strong.

All birds of prey except vultures catch their food. Usually, a hunting bird swoops down and tries to grab the prey with sharp talons. When the prey is caught, the force of impact and the piercing action of the talons are usually enough to kill it instantly. But nine out of ten attacks are unsuccessful. The prey gets away.

A Necessary Skill

In nature, predators are needed. They eliminate insects and vermin as well as animals that are not fit to survive. Birds of prey do their job without cruelty. They are equipped to be efficient and quick. In most cases, the prey does not suffer.

Down feather

Filoplume

Contour feather

Flight feather

Birds of prey usually have large and bright eyes. They have three eyelids to protect their eyes...

Hawks close their eyes most of the time by moving their lower lids up.

Owls move their upper eyelids down —adding to the human appearance of their faces.

The third eyelid, called the nictitating (*NICK-tit-ate-ing*) membrane, closes from side to side. It moistens and cleans the eye.

The size of the talons of a bird of prey depends generally on the size of the prey that must be carried in them.

Barn owls take rats, mice, and other small animals. Their talons are smaller and more delicate.

Harpy eagles have been known to take small sheep, and their talons are as big as the claws of a grizzly bear.

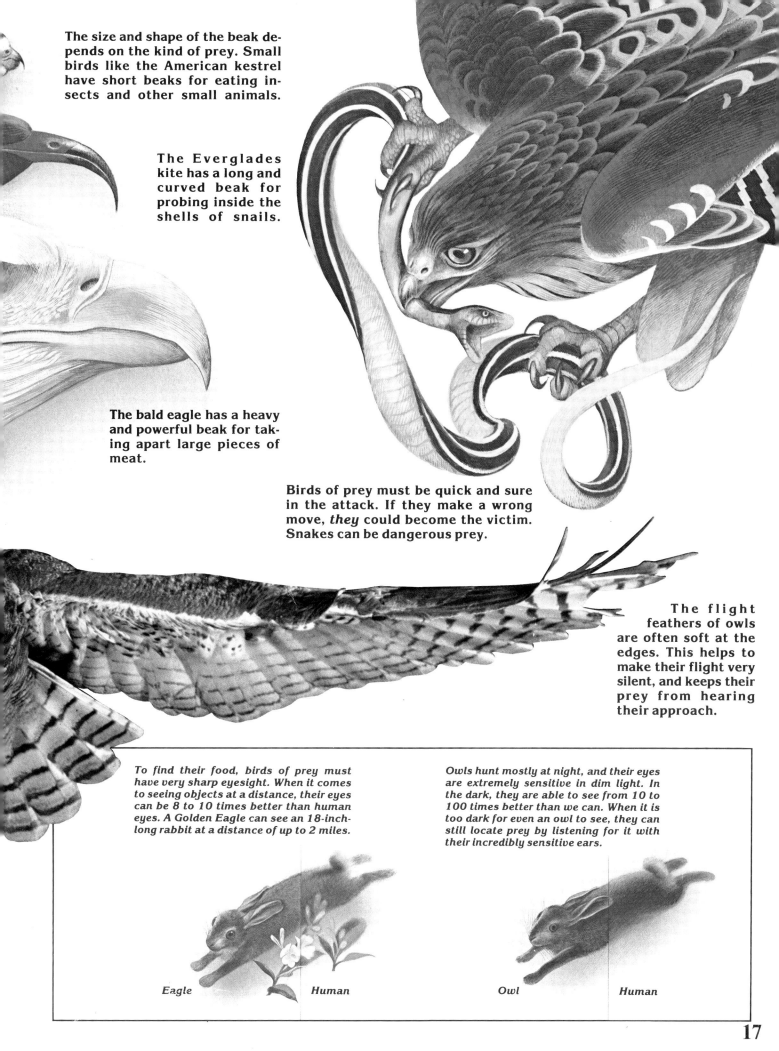

The size and shape of the beak depends on the kind of prey. Small birds like the American kestrel have short beaks for eating insects and other small animals.

The Everglades kite has a long and curved beak for probing inside the shells of snails.

The bald eagle has a heavy and powerful beak for taking apart large pieces of meat.

Birds of prey must be quick and sure in the attack. If they make a wrong move, *they* could become the victim. Snakes can be dangerous prey.

The flight feathers of owls are often soft at the edges. This helps to make their flight very silent, and keeps their prey from hearing their approach.

To find their food, birds of prey must have very sharp eyesight. When it comes to seeing objects at a distance, their eyes can be 8 to 10 times better than human eyes. A Golden Eagle can see an 18-inch-long rabbit at a distance of up to 2 miles.

Owls hunt mostly at night, and their eyes are extremely sensitive in dim light. In the dark, they are able to see from 10 to 100 times better than we can. When it is too dark for even an owl to see, they can still locate prey by listening for it with their incredibly sensitive ears.

Eagle   *Human*

Owl   *Human*

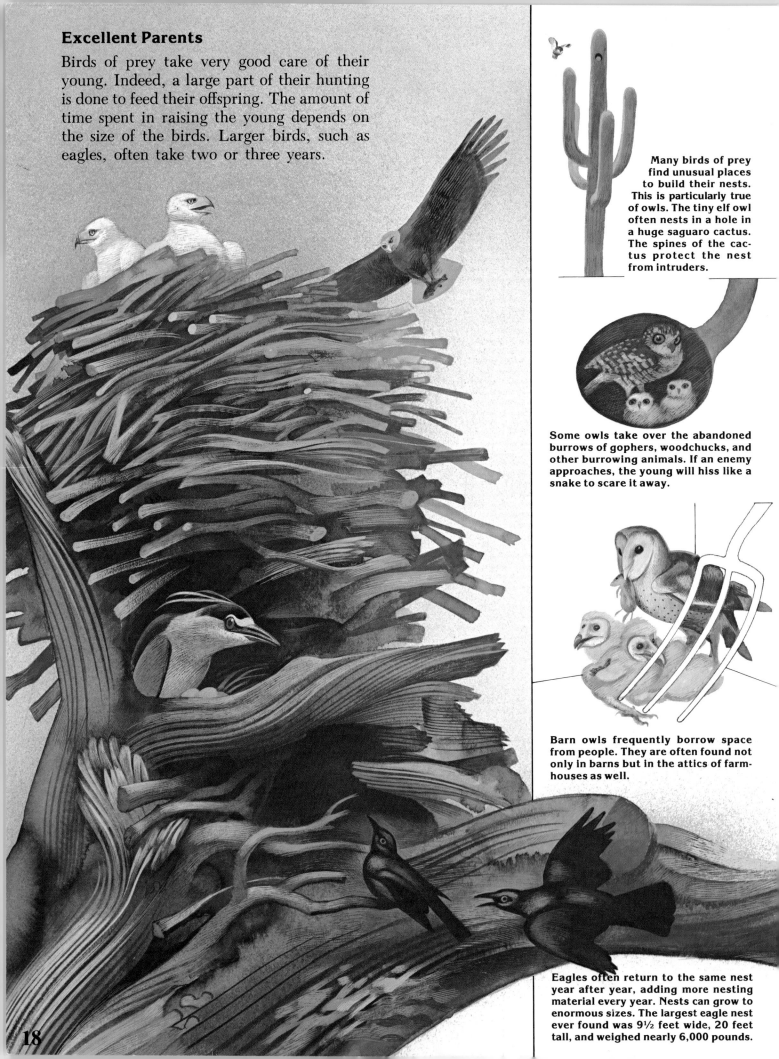

Excellent Parents

Birds of prey take very good care of their young. Indeed, a large part of their hunting is done to feed their offspring. The amount of time spent in raising the young depends on the size of the birds. Larger birds, such as eagles, often take two or three years.

Many birds of prey find unusual places to build their nests. This is particularly true of owls. The tiny elf owl often nests in a hole in a huge saguaro cactus. The spines of the cactus protect the nest from intruders.

Some owls take over the abandoned burrows of gophers, woodchucks, and other burrowing animals. If an enemy approaches, the young will hiss like a snake to scare it away.

Barn owls frequently borrow space from people. They are often found not only in barns but in the attics of farmhouses as well.

Eagles often return to the same nest year after year, adding more nesting material every year. Nests can grow to enormous sizes. The largest eagle nest ever found was 9½ feet wide, 20 feet tall, and weighed nearly 6,000 pounds.

Peregrine Falcon

Gray Sea Eagle

Great Horned Owl

Turkey Vulture

Caracara

The length of time that mated birds of prey stay together is determined by the number of seasons they must spend raising their young. Condors, for example, usually mate for a long time or for life. Smaller birds may stay together for only one season.

Young birds of prey may be heavier than their parents by the time they leave the nest. But when they start hunting on their own, they quickly lose weight. If they do not soon learn to hunt well, the young birds may die.

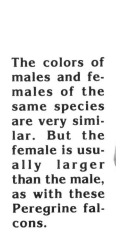

The colors of males and females of the same species are very similar. But the female is usually larger than the male, as with these Peregrine falcons.

The eggs of birds of prey vary greatly in size, shape, color, and texture. Most species lay from one to four eggs, but certain owls may lay as many as a dozen if food is plentiful. The larger birds seldom lay more than two. The female bird keeps the eggs warm until they hatch, while the male bird does the hunting for them both. The eggs above are shown about ⅔ actual size.

19

The Future of Birds of Prey Is Up to Us...

Birds of prey are in danger. Their numbers have been severely reduced over the last few years, because people have been killing them in a variety of ways. Some people feel it is good to shoot and trap birds of prey because they are said to kill a lot of farm animals. But this is a mistaken idea. Birds of prey kill relatively few farm animals.

Hawks sometimes do catch chickens. And eagles do sometimes carry off small farm animals. But the main food of birds of prey are the animals that are the farmer's worst enemies — rats, mice, insects, and other crop destroyers. Birds of prey *help* farmers by killing millions of pests every year. Farmers should protect them.

Pesticides are another great danger to the birds. Often, small animals absorb small quantities of pesticide. The amount may not be enough to kill them, but it stays in their bodies. As birds of prey kill rodents and insects, the amounts of pesticide in their bodies add up. Finally, the total amount is enough to kill the birds.

A third danger is human population. As people convert wild places to farms and housing developments, the hunting territories of the birds are destroyed. The small prey animals are driven out or killed by man. There is little or nothing left for the birds to eat. They leave, or die.

It is not too late to save the birds of prey. We can stop shooting and trapping them. We can stop using the kinds of pesticides that accumulate in the bodies of animals (which would make life healthier for people as well). We can stop destroying wild areas, or relocate birds when their territories have been ruined. And we can find ways to increase the breeding potential of the most severely endangered birds.

Zoos and other animal care organizations have started programs to breed endangered birds of prey. But this will not insure the long-term survival of many species unless we all help to make this world safer for the birds.

Index